VOL. 5

HAL•LEONARD®

VIOLIN

PLAY-ALONG

AUDIO ACCESS INCLUDED

PLAYBACK+
Speed • Pitch • Balance • Loop

Christmas Carols

T0085240

To access audio visit:
www.halleonard.com/mylibrary

Enter Code
4261-5696-4976-5053

Tracking, mixing, and mastering by Jake Johnson
Violin by Jerry Loughney
Guitars by Doug Boduch
Bass by Tom McGirr
Keyboards by Warren Wiegratz
Drums by Scott Schroedl

ISBN: 978-1-4234-1381-3

Visit Hal Leonard Online at www.halleonard.com

HAL•LEONARD®
CORPORATION

7777 W. BLUEMOUND RD. P.O. BOX 13819
MILWAUKEE, WISCONSIN 53213

HAL•LEONARD®
VIOLIN
PLAY-ALONG

AUDIO
ACCESS
INCLUDED

Christmas
Carols

CONTENTS

Angels We Have Heard on High

Traditional French Carol
Translated by James Chadwick

Moderately ♩ = 100

1. An - gels we have heard on high, sweet - ly sing - ing
2. *See additional lyrics*

o'er the plains. And the moun - tains in re - ply, ech - o - ing their

joy - ous strains. Glo

- ri - a in ex - cel - sis De - o.

Glo - ri - a

1.
in ex - cel - sis De - o.
2.
o.

Additional Lyrics

2. Shepherds why this jubilee,
   Why your joyous strains prolong?
   What the gladsome tidings be
   Which inspire your heavenly song?

Away in a Manger

Traditional
Words by John T. McFarland (v.3)
Music by James R. Murray

Additional Lyrics

2. The cattle are lowing, the baby awakes,
   But little Lord Jesus, no crying He makes.
   I love Thee, Lord Jesus, look down from the sky
   And stay by my cradle 'til morning is nigh.

3. Be near me, Lord Jesus, I ask Thee to stay
   Close by me forever and love me I pray.
   Bless all the dear children in Thy tender care
   And take us to heaven to live with Thee there.

Deck the Hall

Traditional Welsh Carol

Additional Lyrics

2. See the blazing yule before us;
   Fa, la, la, la, la, la, la, la, la.
   Strike the harp and join the chorus;
   Fa, la, la, la, la, la, la, la, la.
   Follow me in merry measure;
   Fa, la, la, la, la, la, la, la, la.
   While I tell of Yuletide treasure.
   Fa, la, la, la, la, la, la, la, la.

3. Fast away the old year passes;
   Fa, la, la, la, la, la, la, la, la.
   Hail the new ye lads and lasses;
   Fa, la, la, la, la, la, la, la, la.
   Sing we joyous, all together;
   Fa, la, la, la, la, la, la, la, la.
   Heedless of the wind and weather;
   Fa, la, la, la, la, la, la, la, la.

The First Noël

17th Century English Carol
Music from W. Sandys' *Christmas Carols*

Additional Lyrics

2. They looked up and saw a star
   Shining in the East, beyond them far.
   And to the earth it gave great light
   And so it continued both day and night.

3. And by the light of that same star,
   Three wise men came from country far;
   To seek for a King was their intent,
   And to follow the star wherever it went.

4. The star drew nigh to the northwest,
   O'er Bethlehem it took its rest;
   And there it did both stop and stay,
   Right over the place where Jesus lay.

5. Then entered in those wise men three,
   Full reverently upon their knee;
   And offered there in His presence,
   Their gold, and myrrh, and frankincense.

Go, Tell It on the Mountain

African-American Spiritual
Verses by John W. Work, Jr.

Additional Lyrics

2. The shepherds feared and trembled
   When, lo! above the earth
   Rang out the angel chorus
   That hailed our Savior's birth.

3. Down in a lowly manger
   Our humble Christ was born.
   And God sent us salvation
   That blessed Christmas morn.

Joy to the World

Words by Isaac Watts
Music by George Frideric Handel
Arranged by Lowell Mason

Additional Lyrics

2. He rules the world with truth and grace
And makes the nations prove
The glories of His righteousness
And wonders of His love,
And wonders of His love,
And wonders, wonders of His love.

Jingle Bells

Words and Music by J. Pierpont

Additional Lyrics

2. A day or two ago, I thought I'd take a ride,
   And soon Miss Fannie Bright was sitting by my side.
   The horse was lean and lank,
   Misfortune seemed his lot.
   He got into a drifted bank and we, we got upsot! Oh!

3. Now the ground is white, go it while you're young.
   Take the girls tonight and sing this sleighing song.
   Just get a bobtail bay,
   Two-forty for his speed.
   Then hitch him to an open sleigh and,
   Crack, you'll take the lead! Oh!

O Little Town of Bethlehem

Words by Phillips Brooks
Music by Lewis H. Redner

Additional Lyrics

2. For Christ is born of Mary, and gathered all above.
   While mortals sleep the angels keep
   Their watch of wond'ring love.
   O morning stars, together proclaim the holy birth!
   And praises sing to God the King,
   And peace to men on earth!

HAL•LEONARD
VIOLIN PLAY-ALONG

AUDIO ACCESS INCLUDED

The Violin Play-Along Series

Play your favorite songs quickly and easily!

Just follow the music, listen to the CD or online audio to hear how the violin should sound, and then play along using the separate backing tracks. The audio files are enhanced so you can adjust the recordings to any tempo without changing pitch!

1. Bluegrass
00842152 ....$14.99

2. Popular Songs
00842153 ....$14.99

3. Classical
00842154 ....$14.99

4. Celtic
00842155 ....$14.99

5. Christmas Carols
00842156 ....$14.99

7. Jazz
00842196 ....$14.99

8. Country Classics
00842230 ....$14.99

9. Country Hits
00842231 ....$14.99

10. Bluegrass Favorites
00842232 ....$14.99

11. Bluegrass Classics
00842233 ....$14.99

12. Wedding Classics
00842324 ....$14.99

13. Wedding Favorites
00842325 ....$14.99

14. Blues Classics
00842427 ....$14.99

15. Stephane Grappelli
00842428 ....$14.99

16. Folk Songs
00842429 ....$14.99

17. Christmas Favorites
00842478 ....$14.99

18. Fiddle Hymns
00842499 ....$14.99

19. Lennon & McCartney
00842564 ....$14.99

20. Irish Tunes
00842565 ....$14.99

21. Andrew Lloyd Webber
00842566 ....$14.99

22. Broadway Hits
00842567 ....$14.99

23. Pirates of the Caribbean
00842625 ....$14.99

24. Rock Classics
00842640 ....$14.99

25. Classical Masterpieces
00842642 ....$14.99

26. Elementary Classics
00842643 ....$14.99

27. Classical Favorites
00842646 ....$14.99

28. Classical Treasures
00842647 ....$14.99

29. Disney Favorites
00842648 ....$14.99

30. Disney Hits
00842649 ....$14.99

31. Movie Themes
00842706 ....$14.99

32. Favorite Christmas Songs
00102110 ....$14.99

33. Hoedown
00102161 ....$14.99

34. Barn Dance
00102568 ....$14.99

35. Lindsey Stirling
00109715 ....$19.99

36. Hot Jazz
00110373 ....$14.99

37. Taylor Swift
00116361 ....$14.99

38. John Williams
00116367 ....$14.99

39. Italian Songs
00116368 ....$14.99

40. Trans-Siberian Orchestra
00119909 ....$19.99

41. Johann Strauss
00121041 ....$14.99

42. Light Classics
00121935 ....$14.99

43. Light Orchestra Pop
00122126 ....$14.99

44. French Songs
00122123 ....$14.99

45. Lindsey Stirling Hits
00123128 ....$19.99

46. Piazzolla Tangos
48022997 ....$16.99

47. Light Masterworks
00124149 ....$14.99

48. Frozen
00126478 ....$14.99

49. Pop/Rock
00130216 ....$14.99

50. Songs for Beginners
00131417 ....$14.99

51. Chart Hits for Beginners – 2nd Ed.
00293887.....................$14.99

52. Celtic Rock
00148756 ....$14.99

53. Rockin' Classics
00148768 ....$14.99

54. Scottish Folksongs
00148779 ....$14.99

55. Wicked
00148780 ....$14.99

56. The Sound of Music
00148782 ....$14.99

57. Movie Music
00150962 ....$14.99

58. The Piano Guys – Wonders
00151837 ....$19.99

59. Worship Favorites
00152534 ....$14.99

60. The Beatles
00155293 ....$14.99

61. Star Wars: The Force Awakens
00157648 ....$14.99

62. Star Wars
00157650 ....$14.99

63. George Gershwin
00159612.....................$14.99

64. Lindsey Stirling Favorites
00159634.....................$19.99

65. Taylor Davis
00190208.....................$19.99

66. Pop Covers
00194642.....................$14.99

67. Love Songs
00211896.....................$14.99

68. Queen
00221964.....................$14.99

69. La La Land
00232247.....................$17.99

70. Metallica
00242929.....................$14.99

71. Andrew Lloyd Webber Hits
00244688.....................$14.99

72. Lindsey Stirling – Selections from Warmer in the Winter
00254923.....................$19.99

73. Taylor Davis Favorites
00256297.....................$19.99

74. The Piano Guys – Christmas Together
00262873.....................$19.99

75. Ed Sheeran
00274194.....................$16.99

77. Favorite Christmas Hymns
00278017.....................$14.99

78. Hillsong Worship Hits
00279512.....................$14.99

79. Lindsey Stirling – Top Songs
00284305.....................$19.99

80. Gypsy Jazz
00293922.....................$14.99

HAL•LEONARD®
www.halleonard.com

COMPOSER'S CHOICE

The Composer's Choice series showcases piano works by an exclusive group of composers, all of whom are also teachers and performers. Each collection contains 8 original solos and includes classic piano pieces that were carefully chosen by the composer, as well as brand-new compositions written especially for the series. The composers also contributed helpful and valuable performance notes for each collection. Get to know a new Willis composer today!

CLOSER LOOK

View sample pages and hear audio excerpts online at
www.halleonard.com

f @WillisPianoMusic

◉ willispiano

✗ @WillisPiano

▶ Willis Piano Music

ELEMENTARY

GLENDA AUSTIN
MID TO LATER ELEMENTARY
Betcha-Can Boogie • Jivin' Around • The Plucky Penguin • Rolling Clouds • Shadow Tag • Southpaw Swing • Sunset Over the Sea • Tarantella (Spider at Midnight).
00130168 ....$6.99

CAROLYN MILLER
MID TO LATER ELEMENTARY
The Goldfish Pool • March of the Gnomes • More Fireflies • Morning Dew • Ping Pong • The Piper's Dance • Razz-a-ma-tazz • Rolling River.
00118951 ....$7.99

CAROLYN C. SETLIFF
EARLY TO LATER ELEMENTARY
Dark and Stormy Night • Dreamland • Fantastic Fingers • Peanut Brittle • Six Silly Geese • Snickerdoodle • Roses in Twilight • Seahorse Serenade.
00119289 ....$7.99

WILLIS MUSIC

EXCLUSIVELY DISTRIBUTED BY

HAL•LEONARD®
www.willispianomusic.com

Prices, contents, and availability subject to change without notice.

INTERMEDIATE

GLENDA AUSTIN
EARLY TO MID-INTERMEDIATE
Blue Mood Waltz • Chromatic Conversation • Etude in E Major • Midnight Caravan • Reverie • South Sea Lullaby • Tangorific • Valse Belle.
00115242 ....$9.99

ERIC BAUMGARTNER
EARLY TO MID-INTERMEDIATE
Aretta's Rhumba • Beale Street Boogie • The Cuckoo • Goblin Dance • Jackrabbit Ramble • Journey's End • New Orleans Nocturne • Scherzando.
00114465 ....$9.99

RANDALL HARTSELL
EARLY TO MID-INTERMEDIATE
Above the Clouds • Autumn Reverie • Raiders in the Night • River Dance • Showers at Daybreak • Sunbursts in the Rain • Sunset in Madrid • Tides of Tahiti.
00122211 ....$8.99

NAOKO IKEDA
EARLY TO MID-INTERMEDIATE
Arigato • The Glacial Mermaid • Land of the Midnight Sun • Sakura • Scarlet Hearts (solo version) • Shooting Stars in Summer • Soft Rain (Azisai) • ...You.
00288891 ....$8.99

CAROLYN MILLER
EARLY INTERMEDIATE
Allison's Song • Little Waltz in E Minor • Reflections • Ripples in the Water • Arpeggio Waltz • Trumpet in the Night • Toccata Semplice • Rhapsody in A Minor.
00123897 ....$8.99